Gerbils

MC

Understanding and Caring for Your Pet

Written by
Jackie Roswell

Mason Crest
450 Parkway Drive, Suite D
Broomall, PA 19008
www.masoncrest.com
Developed and produced by Mason Crest

Printed and bound in the United States of America.

First printing
9 8 7 6 5 4 3 2 1

Series ISBN: 978-1-4222-3691-8
ISBN: 978-1-4222-3696-3
ebook ISBN: 978-1-4222-8088-1

Every reasonable care has been taken in the compilation of this publication.
The Publisher and Author cannot accept liability for any loss, damage, injury, or
death resulting from the keeping of gerbils by user(s) of this publication, or from
the use of any materials, equipment, methods, or information recommended in this
publication or from any errors or omissions that may be found in the text of this
publication or that may occur at a future date, except as expressly provided by law.
No animals were harmed in the making of this book.

Words in bold are explained in the glossary on page 127.

QR CODES AND LINKS TO THIRD PARTY CONTENT

Understanding and Caring for Your Pet

 Educational Videos: Readers can view videos by scanning our QR codes, providing them with additional educational content to supplement the text. Examples include news coverage, moments in history, speeches, iconic moments, and much more!

 Words to Understand: These words with their easy-to-understand definitions will increase the reader's understanding of the text, while building vocabulary skills.

Contents

Perfect Pets

Gerbils make wonderful pets and have been popular with families for many years. Here are some of the reasons gerbils are such attractive animals to keep.

- They are clean animals with no odor.
- They are easy to look after and comparatively cheap to buy.
- They are social animals that enjoy human company.
- They are awake during the day, so there is plenty of opportunity to handle and interact with them.
- Health problems are rare.

Their small size—a body of 5-6 inches (12 to 14 cm) and a tail of 3-4 inches (8 to 10 cm)—makes them easy to handle, and they do not need a large amount of space. Their lifespan of three to five years is significantly longer than most other small pet rodents, such as mice and hamsters.

In the wild

There are around 100 species of gerbils, which live in dry grasslands and semi-deserts across Africa, the Middle East, India, and Central Asia.

Gerbils are members of the rodent family. This is the largest group of mammals, and contains over 2,000 different species of varying shapes and sizes. The word rodent comes from the Latin word "rodere," meaning to gnaw, and gnawing is one thing all rodents have in common.

They gnaw to get their food and to make their homes. Rodents have four big front teeth, the **incisors**, evolved for gnawing. These sharp chisel-shaped teeth meet together like pincers and are very effective. They grow continually throughout the animal's life.

Gerbils belong to a family of rodents called the Myomorpha, which also includes mice, rats, hamsters, lemmings, and voles.

The gerbil commonly kept as a pet is a species with the scientific name Meriones unguiculatus but is most often known as the Mongolian Gerbil or the Clawed Jird.

All gerbils are adapted to live in a very dry environment where they have evolved to conserve moisture, and to cope with extremes of heat and cold. With a few exceptions, gerbils are social animals that live in burrows or groups of burrows. They get most of the moisture they need from their food, and although their diet consists mainly of vegetables, they are truly **omnivorous**, eating anything they can find to sustain themselves, including insects.

Opposite:
A Golden Agouti
explores his
surroundings.

The Mongolian Gerbil comes from the semi-desert regions of Mongolia and northern China. They live in extensive burrow systems in family groups of between 12 and 20. There will be a dominant male and female who breed, several males who will help **forage** and defend the territory controlled by the burrow, and younger gerbils being raised. Any older males and females that threaten the dominance of the breeding pair will be driven from the burrow.

The burrow is very important as it provides protection from predators, which for the Mongolian Gerbil is mainly birds of prey, and also provides protection from the climate. Gerbils in the wild live in a very harsh climate. Summer daytime temperatures can exceed 120°F (50 °C) and in winter temperatures can drop as low as -40 °C/F. The differences between day and night can also be extreme. In parts of the Mongolian Gerbil's range 86°F (30 °C) can be reached during the day with temperatures of below 32°F (0 °C) at night.

Living 3 feet (1 m) or more below ground the gerbils can shelter from these extremes. They also store food in special chambers in their burrow, and also drink the moisture that condenses on the cool walls of the tunnels.

The French Connection

In the 19th century a French missionary, Father Armand David, traveled widely in northern and western China, collecting specimens of animals and plants that were unknown to western science. He sent his many discoveries, including the Giant Panda, back to Paris and in 1867 he included specimens of the Mongolian Gerbil, which allowed the species to be scientifically described for the first time.

For many years the species was nothing more than a scientific curiosity, but in 1954 Dr. Victor Schwentker imported gerbils into the United States for use in research. Their suitability as pets was discovered and they were introduced to the pet market. In 1964 they were first imported to Great Britain, too, and are now popular pets available in pet shops throughout most of the world.

Choosing
Your Gerbils

Gerbils are generally active, healthy and easy to handle, however, it is important that you choose animals that do not have health problems. These are the signs of a healthy gerbil:

Choosing the right gerbil for you

- They should be lively, curious, and active. If they are asleep, ask the shop assistant to wake them gently, then watch their reaction. They should quickly wake up and be interested in what is going on around them, with a natural urge to explore and investigate.

- Eyes should be bright and bold with no sign of discharge.

- Check their rear ends to make sure there is no diarrhea or staining.

- Avoid gerbils with the fur sticking up roughly. The coat should be smooth.

- Also avoid any gerbil that sits hunched in a corner and does not investigate the human visitor.

- If possible, get your ear close to the gerbil. There should be no clicking or squeaking sound as he breathes. If there is, it is a sign of a chest infection and the gerbil should be avoided.

Males or females?

It is easy to tell which gender a gerbil is. Males have a distinctive bulge at the base of the tail. This differentiates them from females from about four weeks of age. Even before then it is easy to tell the difference as the two openings at the base of the tail are very close together in females, but much further apart in males.

Gerbils are social animals and need the company of their own kind, so buy a pair of gerbils, rather than a single creature. Go for two males or two females.

Gerbils are social and can live in groups, but it is better to keep just a pair. Large groups can become unstable and aggression can break out. Most fights are due to dominance issues and, while two females usually live happily together, dominance problems are more likely if you keep females.

Gerbils are very territorial when adult and will fight other gerbils who are strangers to them. Up to 8 weeks old, gerbils will mix happily and will settle down with any new gerbils that are introduced. But once the are adults, special care is needed when introducing gerbils. For this reason it is best to get your pair of gerbils from the same place at the same time.

Coat Varieties

Coat varieties

Wild gerbils have a brown coat consisting of hairs which are slate grey at the base, bright yellow in the middle, and black at the tip. The belly is covered with white fur that has dark roots. Wild gerbils have black eyes.

Since gerbils were first introduced as pets several **genetic mutations** have occurred that affect the color of the gerbil's fur or eyes. Breeders have combined those mutations to produce over 20 different varieties of gerbil.

These colors are usually organized as, Selfs, White Bellied, and Other Varieties.

Self colors

Self colored gerbils are the same color all over and, at a gerbil show, would be penalized for having hairs of any other color.

White

These have a completely white coat and come in pink-eyed and ruby-eyed (pictured) varieties.

Black

These gerbils are completely black with black eyes. It is normal for them to have some white hairs, especially on the nose, throat and sometimes on the feet.

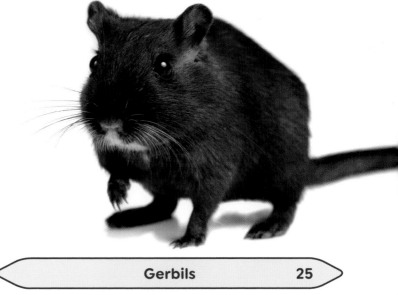

Slate

These are very dark grey all over, almost as dark as a black gerbil, and will usually have similar white markings on the throat, nose, and feet.

Lilac

This color is medium grey all over with ruby colored eyes.

Dove

These look similar to lilac gerbils, but have a very light grey coat.

Pictured:
Pearl (left), Dove (above),
Slate (right).

White bellied

All these gerbils have a white belly with a colored coat for the rest of the body. There should be a clear distinction between the white belly and the main color, except for the honey colors where there is a more gradual boundary between the belly and the top coat.

Golden Agouti

This is the color of gerbils in the wild—a brown coat with white belly and black eyes.

Grey Agouti

Just like a golden agouti but all the yellow color has been stripped from the coat, leaving it grey. Unlike the self grey colors such as lilac, the belly is white, and the grey appearance is not from grey hairs, but from the mixture of white and black pigment.

Argente

These come in two varieties—argente golden, and argente cream. They have the white belly of a golden agouti gerbil, but the fur on their backs is golden yellow and they have ruby colored eyes. Argente cream has white tips to the fur so the coat is lighter and has a silvery sheen.

Pictured:
Argente spot (top),
Grey agouti (middle),
Golden agouti (bottom).

Cream

This is a ruby eyed color that is almost white, but the color on the back is a yellow off-white, and the belly is white.

Honeys

These come in two varieties: Dark-eyed and Red-eyed. They are yellow gerbils that have a white belly that comes half-way up their side and either red or black eyes.

Other varieties

This group of colors has no single distinguishing feature and is a catch-all for various colors which don't fit into the self or white bellied groups.

Himalayan

These gerbils are exactly like a pink-eyed white when born, but as they reach maturity their tail develops grey or brown pigment.

Siamese

These look just like a Siamese cat with a creamy greyish body and dark brown points on the tail, ears, feet, and nose. They have black eyes.

Burmese

These are like a Siamese but much darker. The body color is brown and the points are almost black.

Nutmeg

These unusual gerbils look similar to a dark-eyed honey when young, but as they reach maturity they grow hairs with dark tips so they appear similar in color to a golden agouti but do not have a white belly. The belly is similar to the color on their back, only lighter.

Silver Nutmeg

This is the grey agouti equivalent of the nutmeg. When young, they are creamy yellow in color but when adult they are grey all over, looking like a grey agouti but without the white belly.

Above:
Siamese (top),
Burmese (bottom).

Saffron

This gerbil is golden yellow all over, although the belly is a little lighter than the coat on the back. Unlike the nutmegs, saffrons have red eyes.

Black-Eyed White

These gerbils have black eyes and very light colored fur. They are not truly white as there is always some grey or black tips to the fur, especially on the tail.

Below: Black (left), Siamese spot (right).

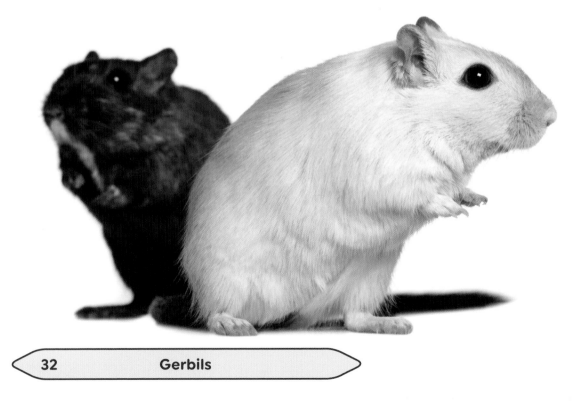

Spotted, Pied, and Mottled

Any gerbil color can have white spots, although obviously you won't be able to see them where the fur is already white. The amount of white varies a lot between gerbils. The white markings come in two types. The first is simply called Spotting and the gerbil will normally have a white nose, a spot on the forehead, a spot on the back of the neck, a white tip to the tail, and, although you can't see it on a white bellied gerbil, a white chest. Pied gerbils have the same markings but distinctly larger amounts of white, so the white spots on the chest, neck and head join up. Pied gerbils often have small patches of white on their back and flanks, too. When these pied markings are so extensive that the gerbil looks like a patchwork of white and color it is known as Mottled.

Below: Golden agouti pied gerbil.

Additional varieties

All the above colors are reasonably common and can be found in pet stores. There are a couple of other varieties which you may come across, although they are much more unusual.

Blue

These gerbils are similar to slate gerbils but the color of the coat is a much warmer blue color.

Rex

Recently gerbils with a wavy rather than straight coat have appeared in Eastern Europe. Although very rare, it is only a matter of time before they become more common. Rex gerbils can be in any of the above colors.

Other Species

Of the 100 species of gerbils, several types other than the Mongolian are kept as pets. Not all are suitable as pets—some species, like the Indian Gerbil (Tatera indica) for example, can be aggressive and difficult to handle. However, most gerbil species are easy to handle and almost never aggressive towards people.

Species other than the Mongolian Gerbil only tend to be available from specialist breeders, although they do sometimes turn up in pet stores. The most common species kept as pets include:

Pallid Gerbil

The Pallid gerbil (Gerbillus perpallidus) lives in the arid areas of North Africa and is sometimes confused with the Egyptian gerbil (G. gerbillus) and Cheesman's gerbil (G. cheesmani) which are different, although very similar, species which can be kept as pets in the same way.

In appearance this gerbil is quite different to the Mongolian gerbil. First, it is smaller. Males are about three-quarters the size of an adult Mongolian while the female is significantly smaller still.

The coloring is both lighter and brighter than that of the agouti colored Mongolian gerbil. The overall effect is much more orange than brown, and the belly is brilliant white. The body and limbs are much more finely boned than the Mongolian gerbil and the tail is much longer, only sparsely haired and with no tuft. Eyes are much larger in proportion to the head, which is much more pointed in shape. The ears are larger and stand more erect.

Pallid Gerbils as pets

Pallids make good pets. In general their habits and temperament are like those of the Mongolian Gerbil. They are social animals, and seem to get bored and depressed when kept alone. They will live quite happily in single sex groups but large groups containing both sexes are sometimes unstable, with occasional outbreaks of violence. In most respects they can be kept in the same manner as Mongolian gerbils.

Shaw's Jird

Shaw's jird (Meriones shawi) is about the same size as a rat and looks like a giant version of the Mongolian gerbil. It originates from the arid areas of North Africa. Sunderval's jird (M. crassus) is a similar species which is smaller but can be kept as a pet in a similar way.

Opposite:
Sundervall's jird.

Shaw's jirds as pets

Shaw's jirds make wonderful pets. They have the same friendliness and natural curiosity as their Mongolian cousins. They rarely bite and enjoy being handled. Being that much bigger, they are easier to cuddle. They are also extremely intelligent. They like to explore and run free, but one problem with giving them the freedom of the room is that they will gnaw at everything. Shaw's jirds have bigger teeth than Mongolian gerbils and are able to cause more damage. It is important to make sure that all electric cables are beyond their reach. Pet jirds should be kept as a pair in the case of males or singly in the case of females, although now that fresh blood has been imported from Egypt, female Shaw's jirds from this line appear to tolerate the company of other females.

Persian Jird

The Persian jird (Meriones persicus) is also large. Although not as well built as a Shaw's jird, it is a little longer, about 6 inches (15 cm) with a tail that is about 15 percent longer than the body. Their coloration is the normal agouti. The belly is a particularly brilliant white. The long tail has a beautiful brush that extends along nearly a third of its length.

Opposite:
Persian Jird.

They come from central Asia including Turkey, Iran, and Afghanistan. In some regions they occupy flat semi-deserts, but their favorite habitat is dry rocky hillsides with little vegetation. They prefer sloping ground and will occupy the rock-strewn mountain gorges cut by seasonal streams and rivers. Although they will dig burrows, these are fairly simple affairs by gerbil standards and have few entrances. Persian jirds will often simply shelter under overhanging rocks.

Persian jirds as pets

Persian jirds love to climb and jump. They are very agile so need an enclosure with plenty of space, as they like to clamber and leap around. They like to have a nest box, but give them several as they may fill the first one with **hoarded** food! In captivity it is fairly easy to reproduce their natural diet with hamster mix, mealworms and/or dry cat food.

They are naturally quite tame, do not bite, seem unafraid of humans and can be handled quite easily. In captivity they have been known to live for six or seven years.

Fat-tailed gerbils (Duprasi)

The Fat-Tailed gerbil (Pachyuromys duprasis), also often called the duprasi, is about 4 inches (10 cm) long with a thick, fluffy coat. It looks rather like a hamster, but with a pointed snout and a fat, almost bald, club-shaped tail from which it gets its common name. The duprasi stores fat in its tail in the same way that the camel stores fat in its hump. Therefore, a healthy duprasi should have a nicely rounded tail.

Although the duprasi belongs to the gerbil family, the gerbillinae, it is not closely related to the Mongolian gerbil. They come from sandy deserts of Egypt and other parts of North Africa. They have to survive with limited access to both food and water, one of the reasons they have evolved to store fat in their tail. They also differ from other gerbil species kept as pets by being much more solitary, and being much more nocturnal.

Fat-tailed gerbils as pets

In general they are best kept in a tank where they can burrow. They like to have a jar, or series of jars, in which they can sleep. They will eat the same food as other gerbils. The sometimes like to have insects such as mealworms or crickets added to their diet but this is not essential. Although they do not drink much, always give them access to water.

Opposite:
Fat tailed gerbil.
Note the thick tail.

The fur is very fine and they don't always look their best when humidity is high. Give them the opportunity to bath in Chinchilla sand every few days to help them keep their fur in good condition.

Duprasi are quite different to Mongolian gerbils in their behavior. While they are still inquisitive, docile and easy to handle, they are much more like hamsters in the way they move about and in their more nocturnal habits. Groups of Duprasi will often live together without trouble but they will sometimes squabble. This can lead to bullying, with the tails of bullied animals being bitten. Often bullying can be resolved by giving each Duprasi his own jar to nest in.

Opposite:
Fat tailed gerbil.

Housing Your Gerbils

The most important factor when choosing a home for your gerbils is size. Allow one square foot (929 sq. cm) of floor space per gerbil and make sure the home is dry, draft proof and secure. It should also accommodate your gerbil's desire to burrow.

Making a safe home
for your gerbil

Opposite:
Lilac gerbil.

Gerbils love to burrow and cannot resist exploring any tubes or holes. It is therefore important that gerbils have a deep tank or multi-level home. Gerbils should have sufficient depth to allow them to burrow and dig around. It is not desirable to let your gerbils dig a large permanent deep burrow system as they will spend most of their time in it, meaning you will find it more difficult to see them and interact with them. They may also become more timid if they are able to run and hide in a burrow when disturbed.

An old fish tank with a secure lid makes a good home for your gerbils, and it doesn't matter if the tank leaks as you won't be keeping water in it! Many pet stores sell purpose-designed gerbillariums, which come in two varieties.

One type is a two piece tank, often with some sort of plastic platform. It makes a good home, but be careful to ensure that the housing does not have any corners or holes the gerbils can get their teeth on to or they will gnaw their way out.

The other type consists of a tank to allow the gerbil to dig and a wire cage complete with ramps to allow them to climb and explore. While these make very good gerbil homes that will satisfy their needs, the gerbils may still kick out the contents of their tank, so creating more mess.

There are several options for bedding materials. Each has its own advantages and disadvantages.

Sawdust

This has very little to recommend it. It is very absorbent, but gerbils do not create much moisture, and sawdust has been known to cause irritation to gerbil eyes and noses.

Wood Shavings

One of the better options. It is clean and does not usually cause problems for the gerbil, but avoid strong-smelling shavings such cedar, or scented shavings as the oils in these materials can cause allergic reactions and eye and breathing problems. Gerbils will tend to chew the shavings as part of their normal nest making activities which causes the pieces to get smaller and hold together well for burrowing. If mixed with cardboard and paper the fibers the gerbils create from shredding these will help bind the shavings, allowing burrows to hold together.

Shredded paper

Very clean, and no risk of allergy or other problems, but in itself paper does not provide a very attractive or gerbil friendly environment. However, paper added to wood shavings helps the gerbils burrow in the shavings, and if you suspect your gerbil is suffering from an allergy or other problem related to bedding material, placing your gerbils on paper bedding can help clear up the problem.

Straw and peat

This can be used to provide a more natural environment for your gerbils. It allows complex burrows to be built, but has many disadvantages. It is heavy, and it can be difficult to get the consistency right—too dry and the gerbils cannot burrow, too damp and it can cause **fungal** infections and chest problems. Unless kept damp, gerbils burrowing will spread a lot of peat dust around, making a lot of mess.

Opposite:
Lunchtime for a
Golden agouti.

There are several types of nesting material sold for small pets. In the wild, gerbils line their nests with fibers that they tear from plants using their teeth. Probably the best nesting material for gerbils is simple plain tissue paper. Your gerbils will very quickly shred it into its pieces so it becomes like cotton wool (cotton). They will line their nest with this soft material, and it will cost you almost nothing while enabling your pets to display their natural nest making behaviors.

Opposite:
Golden agouti (left),
Black pied (opposite).

Feeding

Gerbils come from a very barren dry wilderness and have evolved to survive by not overlooking any possible source of food. They will explore and try out almost any foods, living happily on a diet of dry mix, just a normal hamster or gerbil food, but will enjoy small amounts of other foods.

Hungry gerbils!
Proper feeding tips.

Opposite:
Argente golden
tries an apple.

Gerbils can eat anything you can eat, including small amounts of cooked meat, but tend to prefer dry or crunchy foods. They are particularly fond of oily seeds like sunflower and linseed. They will also eat insects.

What this means for the gerbil keeper is that gerbils should be given a varied diet built around a dry mix, but with small amounts of added treats. Gerbils need less fat in their diet than hamsters, so do not give large numbers of sunflower seeds if the mix already contains some, or your gerbils will get fat.

Ideal treats include dried banana, small amounts of parakeet or canary food, pumpkin seeds, millet sprays, cooked beans, crispy vegetables such as raw broccoli, small amounts of fruit, such as grapes (but break the skin so the gerbil can easily see the moist interior), alfalfa, and hay.

Always give small amounts. Fresh food should be removed as soon as the gerbils lose interest in it as they will tend to bury any that is uneaten.

Better quality feeds developed specifically for gerbils are now increasingly appearing on the market. These are designed to have less fat than hamster mixes, and to include a greater variety of foods interesting to your gerbils.

Although gerbils drink very little and can get most of the water they need from their diet, they thrive much better if given access to water. It is best to use a water bottle, as gerbils have a natural instinct to cover water bowls, probably because in the wild it would be a bad thing to have water in the tunnels of their home.

They can damage plastic bottles and will attempt to climb them. If possible, suspend the bottle from the roof of their home in a way which means they can reach the drinking spout but stops the bottle banging on the sides of the tank and keeps the spout above the level of the shavings.

Opposite:
Gerbil using a water bottle.

Behavior

Gerbils are diurnal, which means they are awake during the day. They tend to alternate periods of activity with periods of rest right around the clock. They tend to wake to investigate whenever there is anything going on around them, and so will adapt their routine around their owners.

They are naturally tame, easy to handle, and inquisitive. It should be perfectly possible to handle a gerbil within a day or two of taking it home. Birds are their natural predators, so they are wary of a hand coming down from above to grab them. It is usually much easier to let a gerbil hop on to your open hand rather than to try and grab or grasp the gerbil from above.

Gerbils have fragile tails that are easily damaged. Never grab a gerbil by its tail, other than to gently but firmly hold the point where the tail joins the body. Instead get both your hands under the body and lift while holding the base of the tail between two of your fingers to stop the gerbil leaping off if startled.

Why do gerbils act the way they do?

Opposite:
A three-week-old baby gerbil.

Gerbils, being social animals, are used to other gerbils being around, so they are used to being disturbed, knocked, and stroked. It is very rare for a gerbil to bite.

Gerbils communicate with one another in several ways. They give each other signals about their dominance and status through scent marking, using the scent gland on their belly, through exchanging chemicals in their saliva, and by grooming one another.

They also communicate by drumming their feet to give alarm when frightened. If a gerbil makes this noise, the other gerbils will retreat into burrows or find some other shelter. There is more than one kind of drumming noise as gerbils use this to signal in other ways. For example, foot drumming is part of the mating ritual.

Opposite:
Grey agouti.

Toys and Play

Toys and play

Like all pets, gerbils should have toys to encourage their natural behaviors. Gerbils love to explore anything new, so change their toys often. You don't need to spend a fortune on keeping gerbils happy. What is more, gerbils will tend to chew anything put in their home, so toys need to be either very strong (for example, glazed ceramics), or very expendable. Anything made of wood will give your gerbils hours of gnawing pleasure, but will not last forever.

On the whole, wooden toys are good. There is a huge range available, but it is easy to make your own from any resin-free, untreated wood. Fruit tree prunings that are free of insecticides are good. Pine cones also make good toys, but make sure they are thoroughly cleaned.

There are also plenty of plastic toys available, but gerbils will always chew plastic. Fortunately they don't swallow the things they chew, but take care that anything plastic that has been damaged does not have sharp edges that could injure your gerbils.

Fun time—ideas for toys and play

Opposite:
Golden agouti
pied gerbil.

One of the cheapest toys, and one that gerbils like best, is cardboard! Gerbils love destroying cardboard tubes, tissue boxes, egg boxes, and packaging.

Gerbils love to explore, and one way of helping them satisfy that urge to allow them free range of a room for a few minutes. The room should be chosen very carefully. Make sure there are no other family pets, such as a cat or dog, in the area. Care should also be taken to ensure that there is no means of escape for your gerbils, such as under the floorboards or through an open door. Also make sure there are no wires or furnishings that could be damaged.

When you want to pick up your gerbil to return him to his home, the easy way to do this is to use a cardboard or plastic tube about 12 inches (30cm) long. The gerbil will be drawn to explore it, and, once he is inside, you can put your hands over each end and pick it up.

An alternative to allowing your gerbil to explore a room is to provide him with a large box with various toys and objects for it to explore. That way he will be easier to catch and less likely to injure himself or damage anything.

Exercise

Some gerbils enjoy using an exercise wheel, but many seem to get bored with them and prefer to get their exercise digging. If you use a wheel, always get an enclosed wheel as the traditional mouse wheel designs of open wires can result in injuries, such as a broken tail. An enclosed hamster ball can also be used, but the gerbils seem aware that they are trapped in something and may find this stressful, or simply won't move. If you use one, do so only for a few minutes at a time, and make sure your gerbil is not left unsupervised.

Another ways of exercising your gerbil and interacting with him is to handle him and let him explore your hands and arms. As he becomes more familiar with you he will tend to clamber about more adventurously and will climb on your shoulders and even your head.

Don't worry about your gerbil jumping off you. Gerbils do not have great distance vision, so will normally only jump into space when they are frightened, or if they have explored everything and are bored!

Gerbils keep themselves clean but their fur can get greasy.

In the wild, the dry sandy environment in which they live helps keep their fur dry and in condition. This means that gerbils very much enjoy having access to a dust bath, and it will help your gerbils look better and feel more comfortable.

All you need is a container with sides of about 2 inches (5 cm) with about 0.5 inches (1cm) depth of Chinchilla sand, which you can buy from your local pet store.

If you leave it in their home, your gerbils will tend to use a dust bath as a litter tray, so only offer it for short periods so they can condition their coat. Any droppings will be hard and dry and can easily be removed so the dust bath can be reused.

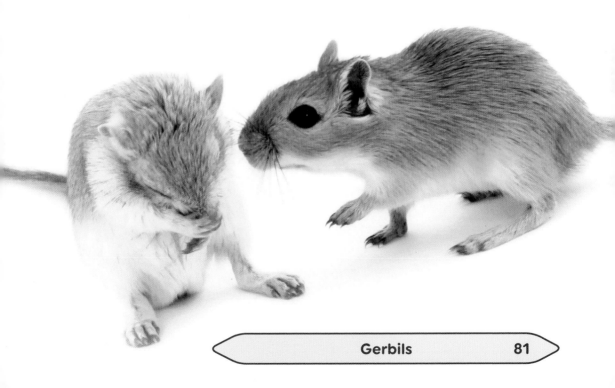

Breeding and Genetics

Pictured: A baby gerbil approximately two weeks old.

Breeding
and Genetics

Before deciding to breed, consider what you are going to do with the young. A pair of gerbils will produce about 50 babies during their reproductive life time.

Gerbils become sexually mature at about four months of age. If you pair up an adult with a younger female, then you may find that she becomes sexually mature slightly younger. Females tend to come into season in the early evening and mating is a noisy and prolonged affair with much drumming of feet, chasing around, and the male repeatedly mating with the female.

After a wait of 21—25 days the mother will give birth. There is often no sign she is pregnant, although her belly may appear slightly swollen for the last two or three days before birth.

Her behavior may also change, with the male being made unwelcome in the nest shortly before the birth. Gerbil mothers need no help giving birth, and usually

Opposite:
A mixed litter of baby gerbils developing their coats.

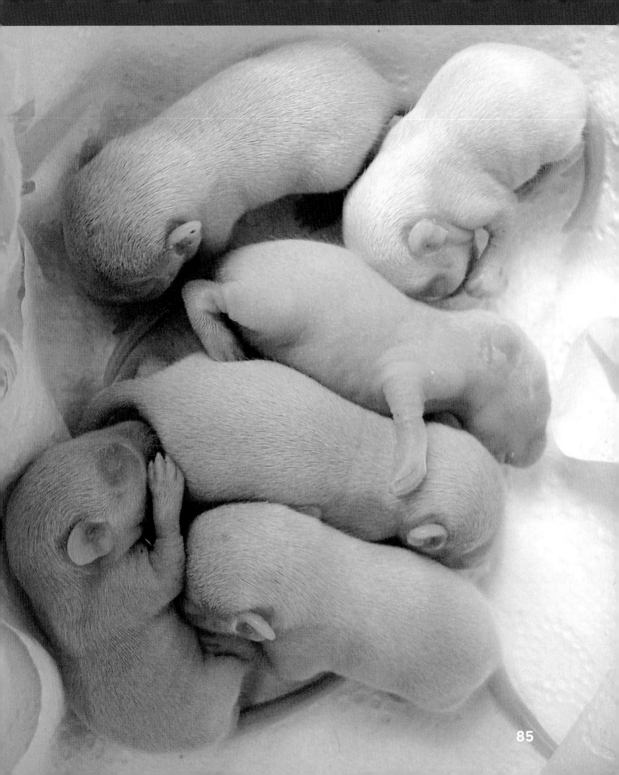

the first sign of the arrival of the litter is the squeaking noise the pups make.

Like many other rodents, gerbils will mate the same day they give birth. However, whilst nursing her pups the implantation of the embryos is delayed so the second litter will usually appear between 28 and 43 days after the birth of the first litter.

Gerbils normally give birth to five or six young, but anything from three to nine is normal. In rare cases where the female only has one or two babies there may not be enough stimulus for the mother to raise them and they often die in a day or two.

The mother often appears to mistreat the pups. She will move them around a lot, split them into two groups, kick them around while digging, etc. This is all perfectly normal and the pups are very rarely harmed. Every now and again she will gather the pups together and feed them. If the father is also in the home he will help care for the pups. He will keep them warm and clean, and can sometimes be seen gathering them up and putting them back in the nest as they start crawling out to explore!

When the pups are born they are pink, hairless, and their eyes and ears are sealed.

All they can do is squeak, wriggle and suckle. They cannot regulate their own temperature and are

dependent on their parents for everything, including being kept warm.

By day three or four their ears open, and fur begins to appear as a light fuzz. You can start to see clues as to the coloration or markings the gerbil will have at this stage.

When the pups are about seven days old they will be much larger than when born. They will have a fur coat thick enough for you to be able to tell what color they are.

By day nine, the pups will start moving around their home exploring. Their eyes will not be open yet, so they tend to move around blindly, often with the parents trying to continually shoo them back into the nest.

Finally at day 17 or 18 the eyes will open, and for the first time the pups will stop looking like newborn dogs, and will at last look like small gerbils. About this time the pups will have developed teeth and will start trying to chew on cardboard, wood shavings and pieces of food. At this stage they are still completely dependent on the mother's milk.

When the pups are about four weeks old they will be regularly eating solid food and will be drinking from the water bottle and will soon stop suckling.

Raising pups usually requires no human intervention. Gerbils make excellent parents, but sometimes, when

the babies are about four weeks old and no longer suckling, they can suffer with a respiratory disorder, whereby the breathing becomes labored and a clicking sound is heard as they breathe. The pup may also appear listless and the fur will be puffed up.

This is probably due to their immature immune system making them susceptible to an infection. This can normally be treated successfully with antibiotics, but it is important to seek veterinary treatment as soon as there are signs of illness.

To ensure your pups complete their social and emotional development they should not be separated from their parents until they are at least six weeks old, by which time they are fully independent. The pups can be kept with the parents until eight weeks old.

The babies won't breed at that age as only the dominant gerbils in the group will normally breed, and that will still be the parents. In the wild, the youngsters will be encouraged to leave the burrow in search of territory of their own. They cannot do this in captivity, so it is important to remove the pups from their parents before any conflict can occur.

Opposite:
Young gerbils aged
around five weeks old.

Gerbil genetics

The color of a gerbil's coat depends on the genes it carries. Each characteristic depends on the code carried in the **chromosomes** in each cell. The point of the chromosome that denotes a characteristic is known as a locus. As chromosomes exist in pairs then each locus will consist of a point on each chromosome of the pair. At these points several different genes can exist that work like switches, turning on or off the relevant characteristics. Every gerbil inherits one chromosome from its mother and one from its father, and every parent will pass on one of each pair of genes to each of its offspring. At each locus there may be one possibility, two, or in some cases three or more. Loci and genes are usually denoted by a letter to indicate the characteristic that is carried at that point.

Opposite:
Agente golden (left),
Black (top), and Golden
agouti (right).

The following loci are known to exist in gerbils:

- **A:** The Agouti Locus, which controls the white belly and the mix of yellow and black pigment in each hair.

- **C:** The Albino Locus, which controls the overall level of color produced, rather like the contrast control on a TV.

- **D:** The Dilute Locus, which controls the depth of color, rather like the brightness control on a TV.

- **E:** The Extension Locus, which controls the balance between black and yellow pigment in the coat.

- **G:** The Grey Locus, which controls the intensity of yellow in the coat.

- **P:** The Pink-Eye Dilution Locus, which controls eye color and whether the coat is lightened.

- **Sp:** The Spotting Locus. This controls white spotting and by default is not referred to unless a gerbil is spotted.

Letters are used to denote the genes at each locus. An upper case letter is used to denote a dominant gene, and a lower case letter is used to denote a recessive gene. For example, at the A locus a gerbil can have one of three combinations—AA, Aa, or aa.

AA and Aa will be the normal golden agouti color of the wild gerbil with hairs that have yellow and black bands and a white belly. If the gerbil is aa it will be completely black.

Any offspring this gerbil has will have a 50/50 chance of inheriting one of the two genes at each locus. So if the gerbil was AA, any offspring would inherit A, if it was aa all offspring would inherit a, but if it was Aa, each pup would have an even chance of either inheriting A or a. The same principle applies for each locus. This principle can be used to work out the likely offspring from a mating, and can also be used to work out from the offspring, what the likely parentage is. For example, if two Golden Agouti parents breed and give birth to Golden agouti pups, but one of the pups is black, the parents must both be Aa to allow the pup to inherit a from both parents.

White spotting is controlled by a locus that operates differently to all the others. There are three things that control spotting, and the pattern of spots.
These are –

- **1) Sp.** This is a dominant gene, and a gerbil that inherits Sp from one parent will be spotted. However, no gerbil is SpSp as that is a fatal combination and gerbils that are SpSp never develop in the womb.

- So all spotted gerbils have one Sp gene and all their offspring will have a 50/50 chance of inheriting spotting from the parent.

- **2) Modifying genes.** There are a number of modifying genes which will tend to mean a gerbil has more or less white spotting. There are possibly dozens of genes which control this, so spotting can take a wide variety of patterns. If the gerbil does not have Sp, the modifying genes will tend to modify any other white markings—for example, the white bars on the hands and the throat that black gerbils often have.

- **3) Pure Chance.** If a gerbil carries Sp, even with the modifying genes having effect, the exact extent of, and pattern of, white spotting is very much down to chance. Two gerbils with identical modifying genes would not have exactly the same pattern of spotting.

Health Care

Gerbils are naturally very robust and are seldom ill. They are not prone to many common illnesses and, unlike some other small animals, rarely suffer with tumors. However, if your gerbil does fall ill, or even seems under the weather, then prompt veterinary attention will ensure the best diagnosis, treatment, and recovery.

Gerbil health care basics

Common problems

Overgrown teeth

This can occur in gerbils that have lost one of the front incisor teeth or in older gerbils that don't tend to chew as much as their younger counterparts. It is usually first identified when the gerbil begins to lose weight. To prevent the problem you should regularly examine the gerbil's teeth. Your vet will be able to trim the teeth for you using a dental tool and it is not painful for the gerbil. Later, once you have seen how it is done, you may even be able to do this yourself, although care needs to be taken not to shatter the tooth and shatter the root. Older gerbils can also lose their teeth. In some cases the teeth will regrow, but if there is a tooth remaining, then this may need to be trimmed to ensure that it does not overgrow.

Overgrown claws

This is usually only a problem with older gerbils due to them not digging as much. An emery board can be used to file the nails down, or if the gerbil is relatively calm and remains still, they can be very careful clipped using nail clippers.

Fits

Some gerbils are prone to having fits. In most cases this is due to stress—for example, being in strange surroundings or getting excessive handling—and generally occurs in younger gerbils. The gerbil starts to twitch, the ears go back and the gerbil may drool at the mouth. If this should happen replace the gerbil in its cage immediately and remove the cage to a quiet area. Within a few minutes the gerbil will recover. Gerbils prone to fits generally grow out of them so the frequency becomes less as time goes by.

Do not breed from affected individuals as it can be passed down from generation to generation. It can be distressing for owners to witness these fits. However, provided you follow the above instructions, your gerbil should recover fully.

In extremely rare cases gerbils have died from a fit, but this may have been caused by some other ailment, such as a brain tumor.

Sore nose

This is quite a common complaint. Usually the cause is allergy. Gerbils are easily irritated by the aromatic oils produced by cedar shavings and many are also allergic to pine.

Sore noses can also be caused by transferring Staphylococci bacilli, one of the causes of sore throats in humans, to gerbils. Your vet can prescribe antibiotic ointment, which needs to be smeared on the nose. This process can often lead to a battle of wills between owner and gerbil!

Gerbils kept in a cage will very often get sore noses. This is because the gerbil will chew constantly at the bars, very often rubbing all the fur off around the nose at the same time. You can prevent this by housing your gerbil in an old aquarium instead.

Sore eyes

This is less common. One of the causes is sawdust, which can get into the **membranes** of the eye and cause irritation. The gerbil will produce copious quantities of red mucous. Treatment is in the form of antibiotic drops from your vet. Switch to wood shavings and follow the advice above on avoiding substances that are known to cause allergies in gerbils.

Opposite:
Grey agouti.

Sore ears

Gerbils will often injure their ears by excessive clean-ing. They clean their ears with the long claws of their back feet and can sometimes damage themselves. If you suspect mites, your gerbil will need treatment.

Gerbils will sometimes have a benign pink growth on the ear that can grow quite fast. If the gerbil catches this when cleaning it can also bleed. These growths are harmless and do not need to be removed unless they grow so big as to block the ear canal.

Loss of tail

A gerbil's tail is quite fragile and rough handling can cause the tuft to come away. Very often the bone will be left behind. While it does not look very pleasant, the bone will dry out, fall off after a few days, and the end will heal over naturally. I have come across cases where an entire tail has been pulled off. In these cases it is better to get the gerbil examined by a vet to check that no other damage has been caused. The gerbil will learn to adapt to the loss and will hardly notice its injury.

Opposite:
Argente golden.

Respiratory illness

Symptoms are a dull coat and breathing that is very obviously laboured, often accompanied by clicking sounds. You should seek veterinary advice.

Diarrhea

Diarrhea can be a sign of Tyzzer's Disease, which attacks the intestines and colon, often proving fatal. If a gerbil show signs of listlessness and diarrhea then it is important that you isolate him. You should then seek veterinary help so that you can treat all your gerbils with antibiotics. Make sure that you thoroughly clean everything, including your hands, that come in contact with the sick gerbils. Not all gerbils with Tyzzer's Disease will exhibit diarrhea as it is only one of many symptoms, including paralysis. Other causes of diarrhea in gerbils are Listeria and Salmonella. These should be treated in the same way as Tyzzer's Disease. Both can be passed on to humans and in some circumstances can be serious, so diarrhea in gerbils should never be ignored.

Mites and other parasites

These are quite rare in gerbils and easily treated. The most common cause is using hay as bedding. Once mites have been identified, then they are very easy to treat and it is possible to buy drops from pet shops which will not only treat mites, but also fleas and other external parasites. More serious **infestation** may require some additional treatment from your vet.

Opposite:
Black pied gerbil.

Inner ear problems

More common in older gerbils, and recognizable when the gerbil has a head tilt. This is caused principally by a **cyst** in the ear. These cysts are common in gerbils and are untreatable. However, my experience is that the chronic condition which causes the gerbil to lose balance and circle while holding its head at an unusual angle, is treatable. Presumably this is caused by an infection that is secondary to the cyst. The best treatment is an anti-inflammatory injection administered by your vet, and a course of antibiotics.

In the most of cases a reduced head tilt remains even though the chronic phase of the condition has passed, but your gerbil will adapt to this and will enjoy life as much as he ever did. Be aware that this problem can reoccur.

If the chronic phase of this condition is not treated then the gerbil will often become totally incapable of caring for itself. It will collapse and quickly die.

Fighting

Sometimes gerbils will injure one another by fighting. The injuries will usually consist of bites to the tail, rump, and bottom area of the losing gerbil. There may also be bites to the face and throat. Not all the bites will be obvious as they are often hidden under the fur.

If one of your gerbils is injured like this it will normally recover on its own if it is eating and drinking. The wounds almost never get infected. If you find it immobile and cold it is necessary to warm it up with a heated pad or hot water bottle. You may need to encourage it to drink. If it has not picked up in a few hours you should seek veterinary help.

If a pair of gerbils that have lived happily together for a long time suddenly fight, the loser may have another illness or injury that has weakened it and lead to its dominance being overthrown.

Opposite:
Grooming helps to reinforce the bond between gerbils.

Illness in Old Age

Strokes

These are recognizable by paralysis or weakness down one side. The best treatment is to try and make the gerbil as comfortable as possible and keep him warm. In some cases another stroke follows fairly soon after and the gerbil may die. Recovery is possible in other cases and the gerbil may be left with little or no disability. The important thing is to make sure the gerbil can feed and drink until it recovers enough to do this itself. If you are concerned seek veterinary advice.

Scent gland tumors

There is a large, dry-looking area of skin on the belly of adult gerbils that secretes a sebum-based scent. This is used by gerbils to mark their territory, allows gerbils to know where others that are part of their group have been, and also help gerbils communicate their relative dominance.

More dominant gerbils will be seen rubbing their bellies on all the objects in their home. Sometimes this gland gets ulcerated or inflamed. This is usually the first sign of a scent gland tumor. These are not normally aggressive and usually stay confined to the scent gland area. Usually the best course is to have your vet remove this. The procedure, under anaesthetic, is not without risk, but has a high success rate and the tumor does not normally return if the surgery is carried out as soon as the problem is identified.

Tumors can also occur in other parts of the body. Again, these can be removed, but there is no guarantee that the tumors will not re-occur.

Heart failure

A gerbil with heart failure may have labored breathing and swelling in the abdominal area due to build up of fluid. It is best to seek advice from a vet, who may be able to draw off the excess fluid and make the gerbil more comfortable.

Ovarian cysts

Sometimes older female gerbils display a swollen abdomen which can look like pregnancy or a bulge on one side. This is normally an ovarian cyst. These can get very large, but are usually harmless and can be ignored. There can be problems if the cyst presses against a nerve or organ and stops it working properly.

If your gerbil appears to be less active than normal or otherwise unwell consult your vet. It may be possible to remove the affected ovary, but this is a major procedure and your vet will be best placed to advise you of the options in each case.

Below: Typical pose of a gerbil affected by a seizure.

Showing gerbils

Showing gerbils is great fun and a very good way of meeting other gerbil fans, to chat, swap information and renew friendships. But, first of all, how do you get started? Who do you need to contact to put in entries? What information do you need to give them? What are the rules? How are the gerbils being judged? The list of questions can be quite daunting.

Many small animal clubs have classes for gerbils and each will have its own rules and procedures. This means the best thing is to get in touch with whoever will be running the show and get as much information as possible.

In general, gerbils can be shown in a small container that will keep the animals secure, and allow them to be observed. The judge will need to be able to open the container and handle and inspect the gerbils.

Shows usually have two types of classes. Breed classes are judged on cleanliness, size, and condition and how well the gerbil complies with a specified standard for each color of gerbil. For example, there will be breed classes for white gerbils, and breed classes for black gerbils. The other type of class will be for pets. The gerbils in the pet class or classes will be judged on cleanliness, size, and condition and not on the relevant color standard.

There will also be classes for new colors that do not have a standard, and often for other species of gerbil that are kept as pets.

Entries can usually be made by mail, telephone, or email. Email is usually best as it both minimizes the risk of misunderstanding or confusion and allows confirmation of receipt, clarification, and correction to be made easily.

If the rules allow you to enter more than one gerbil in a pen, it is important that the judge can tell them apart. For example, they will need to be different colors or different sexes. In the pen you should have shavings and/or paper. Hay should be avoided as it will stain your gerbils and make them appear yellowish. There should also be a small amount of food and, in case your gerbil needs moisture, a small piece of apple or cucumber. Do not use a bottle, or anything that might stain your gerbil.

Gerbils require very little in the way of show preparation, being naturally very clean. But, after a long journey, in their show pens they may be a little greasy. You can freshen them up by using a little Chinchilla sand, which will remove any grease from the fur. All you need to do is to gently sprinkle a little along the back and gently brush it off. The gerbil will groom the rest of it out of the fur and remove the grease in the process. Stains on lighter colored gerbils can be removed by using a little grooming powder or dry shampoo. Strong smelling talc should be avoided.

Judging usually takes two or three hours, but can take longer in a large show. The judge will remove each gerbil from its pen, inspect it and rank the gerbils within each class. With good fortune you will be successful and receive award cards if your gerbil is first, second, or third in any class.

It is a great opportunity for finding out more about gerbils and many lasting friendships are made through meeting people at gerbil shows.

Show places

The American Gerbil Society sponsors three shows annually across the United States, one in New England, one in the Mid-Atlantic region near Washington DC, and a third which moves from city to city across a large swathe of the Midwest. Each show draws members from all over the country, some of whom drive hundreds of miles to participate. The shows have a "family reunion" feel among this close-knit but far-flung group of gerbil enthusiasts. Between shows, AGS members stay in touch through an active email list and various social media. Members have also worked together to rescue scores of gerbils that have found themselves without a home.

Find Out More

Books

Alderton, David. *Looking After Small Pets*. London: Southwater Publishing, 2013.

Fox, Sue. *Gerbils: Animal Planet Pet Care Library*. TFH Publications, 2011.

Web Sites

www.ags.org
The American Gerbil Society has information about gerbil shows, as well as how to find good breeders in your area, plus information about gerbil care.

www.petgerbils.org
Find more links about gerbils as pets along with handy care sheets.

www.aspca.org
The American Society for Prevention of Cruelty to Animals provides information about animals and pets of all kinds.

 # Words to Understand

chromosomes genetic material that passes on physical traits

cyst a liquid-filled growth on an animal

forage search for food

fungal having to do with fungus

genetic mutations unusual changes in an animals' genes over time

hoarded stored away, usually in bulk

incisors the large front teeth of mammals

infestation a large influx or gathering of pests

jird another word for some species of gerbil

membranes thin, usually transparent, coverings of tissue over another body part

omnivorous able to eat and survive on any kind of animal or vegetable matter

Index